CARTER G. WOODSON

THE MAN WHO PUT "BLACK" IN AMERICAN HISTORY

BY JIM HASKINS AND
KATHLEEN BENSON

ILLUSTRATED BY MELANIE REIM

The Millbrook Press • Brookfield, Connecticut

TO J.J. AND NIGEL

Photographs used in art montages courtesy of The Schomburg Center, New York
Public Library: cover; The Metropolitan Museum of Art, Gift of Charles Stewart
Smith, 1884. (84.12c): p. 19; Library of Congress: p. 35 (both)

Library of Congress Cataloging-in-Publication Data
Haskins, James, 1941-
Carter G. Woodson: the man who put "Black" in American history / by Jim Haskins
and Kathleen Benson; illustrated by Melanie Reim
p. cm.
Includes bibliographical references and index.
Summary: A biography of the son of former slaves who received a Ph.D. in history
from Harvard and devoted his life to bringing the achievements
of his race to the world's attention.
ISBN 0-7613-1264-1 (lib. bdg.)
1. Woodson, Carter Godwin, 1875–1950—Juvenile literature.
2. Afro-American historians—Biography—Juvenile literature. 3. Historians—
United States—Biography—Juvenile literature. 4. Afro-
Americans—Historiography—Juvenile literature. [1. Woodson, Carter Godwin,
1875–1950. 2. Historians. 3. Educators. 4. Afro-Americans—Biography.]
I. Benson, Kathleen. II. Reim, Melanie, ill. III. Title.
E175.W65H37 2000 973'.0496073'007202—dc21 [B] 99-53912 CIP AC

Published by The Millbrook Press, Inc.
2 Old New Milford Road
Brookfield, Connecticut 06804
www.millbrookpress.com

CONTENTS

ART NOTES

For tens of thousands of years, artists have been unable to resist the temptation to paint on walls. What began on prehistoric cave walls and continued in ancient Egyptian pyramids is now, at the turn of the twentieth century, being carried on in urban communities. Contemporary artists seem to sense that a story told on a public wall is an ideal forum for social and political statements.

The illustrations for this book are painted as if they are modern murals. The paintings might have appeared in any one of the many communities whose members have benefited from Woodson's heritage. Each one of the six illustrations portrays a significant aspect of Carter G. Woodson's story. Together they serve as a memorial to his achievements.

Each "mural" is painted as if it were actually on a wall. Along the bottom of each one, you will see people looking up, thinking about the story being told, sometimes pointing as if to educate the children, as Woodson educated us.

• **Chapter I: SON OF SLAVES** • Young Carter G. Woodson experienced the laws of segregation growing up in the South. As you look at what appears to be trees and foliage in the center of the painting, you will see a hand held out in the STOP! position preventing black and white people from attending church together. The blacks and whites diverge and follow their separate paths to worship. The white peoples' church is on a hill. Their grass is manicured and their garden is pretty. The railroad running in the background, perhaps the basis of the wealth of many of the whites, was probably built by many of the black men attending church.

• **Chapter II: TEACHER** • The huge ship, books aboard, indicates the vast total of human knowledge — and the huge responsibility of a teacher to pass along that knowledge accurately. Woodson looks very small in relation to the task ahead of him. The big talking head is the missionary who gave Woodson the one idea that directed his life and

4

showed him how he could apply his Filipino experience to the education of black Americans. The Filipinos are on their island in the sea, awaiting the chance to learn to govern themselves.

• Chapter III: FIRST BLACK PH.D. • Carter G. Woodson's lofty educational goals were not easily obtained, as shown by the long ladder of learning that he had to climb to reach the pinnacle. The building represents The Library of Congress. Behind him is the ghost of an injured black Civil War soldier, the symbol of his dawning realization that the real history of his people's contributions to society was not being taught, even in black schools.

• Chapter IV: PUTTING BLACK HISTORY "ON THE MAP" • This mural represents the many voices that *The Journal of Negro History* planned to represent. With the fires of the Klu Klux Klan behind them, Woodson encouraged not only historians, but all of his people, to create written documentation of their history in America. This mural shows just three of the many kinds of voices that came forward — a woman whose clothing indicates her attachment to her African roots, an old man representing the black American past, and a young man who will be the future. They hold their written documents and are speaking out to their community, each with a valid story to tell.

• Chapter V: FOUNDER OF NEGRO HISTORY WEEK • The sun beats down on black children toiling in cotton fields – and the same sun lights the way as children head off to school to learn. Above both scenes, as if keeping watch, hang the images of the two of Woodson's heroes in the struggle for African-American freedom: Frederick Douglass and Abraham Lincoln.

• Chapter VI: FATHER OF AFRICAN-AMERICAN HISTORY • The Civil Rights movement was launched and the floodgates were opened. Blacks were at last able to express themselves publicly, not just in regard to their history, but to their present status and their future prospects as well. The wounded soldier appears again, to represent the way things used to be — before Carter G. Woodson. The other placards represent just two of the many areas in which blacks have excelled: Billie Holiday, who is an important figure in African-American cultural heritage and Jesse Owens, who transcended racism in the Olympics to become a champion.

Melanie Reim

INTRODUCTION

Every February, students across the United States learn about Martin Luther King, Jr., Rosa Parks, George Washington Carver, and other important black people in history. But few students learn about Carter G. Woodson, the "Father of African-American History." Carter G. Woodson started Negro History Week back in 1926. Since then, Negro History Week, which was later renamed Black History Week, has been expanded to become Black History Month. Of course, African-American history ought to be studied at all times of the year. But for many years history books hardly mentioned blacks except when talking about slavery. These books left out most of the important things that black people have done to build our country. Having a spe-

6.

cial Black History Month guarantees that the contributions of black people will be studied for at least one month out of the year.

African Americans are not the only Americans who were left out of history books. The gifts to America by other minority groups and women have also been largely ignored until recent years. Since Black History Month began, special months have been set aside for learning about the contributions of many other groups, including Puerto Rican Heritage Month in November and Asian-Pacific Heritage Month in May.

The only way to know history is to know the whole story. If history books only tell part of it, then no one learns enough. All Americans need to know that people of their gender or ethnic background have been an important part of the history of their country. Today, most history books try to tell the whole story. But that was not always so.

CHAPTER I

SON OF SLAVES

Carter Godwin Woodson was the son of slaves who had been granted their freedom at the end of the Civil War. Born in Virginia in 1875, just ten years after the War Between the States ended with a Union victory, Carter was one of seven children. Although his family owned their own farm, they were quite poor. In a June 25, 1932, article in the Baltimore *Afro-American* newspaper, Carter recalled that his mother struggled to feed her children and often "had her breakfast and did not know where she would find dinner." Carter only had one garment. Often, he had to go to bed early on Saturday night so his mother could wash and iron it for Sunday school the next morning.

As a child, Carter's mother, Anne Eliza Woodson, had been taught to read by her mistress. During the eight months of the year when the whole family was needed on the farm, she taught her children as best she could at home. In the four months of winter, the children attended a one-room school. James Henry Woodson, Carter's father, never learned to read or write. But he taught his children some important lessons about living in a world where many whites considered blacks less than human.

In the world of young Carter G. Woodson, blacks had to stay apart from whites. This was called segregation. Segregation was the law in the South. Blacks could not go to the same churches or schools as white people. The churches and schools for blacks were not as good as those for whites. Blacks had to call whites Mr. and Mrs. and Miss. Whites called even elderly blacks by their first names. It was hard for young black children to feel proud of themselves. But Carter's father taught his children to be proud. He taught them to be polite to everyone, but never to accept insults from whites.

Carter's father would tell his children stories about the war, when he was a slave trained as a carpenter. His master hired him out to work for other people. During the war he was working for a cruel man named James Stratton, who made him dig ditches and worked him hard all day. In the evenings, James Henry

Woodson would carve small items, like fish traps, to sell for pocket change. Stratton saw him working for himself and tried to whip him. But James Henry Woodson whipped Stratton. He then went back to his master's place. When his master said he had to go back to Stratton, James Henry Woodson ran away.

By this time, Union troops were in the Virginia countryside. James Henry Woodson made his way to where those troops were camped. He told of his treatment by James Stratton and then led some of the soldiers to Stratton's place, where they tied up Stratton and whipped him.

James Henry Woodson spent the rest of the war with the Union troops. He led them to mills and supply depots in the county, where they stole supplies and buried whatever they could not carry. He served as a combat soldier in many of the battles in the Virginia countryside. Finally, Confederate General Robert E. Lee surrendered, and the bloody Civil War ended.

James Henry Woodson told his children that other blacks had fought with the Union troops. But the Woodson children did not learn anything about this at school. In fact, they were not taught anything about blacks in history, except that they had been slaves. Carter G. Woodson wondered why.

During the 1880s, Carter's two oldest brothers left the family farm and went to West Virginia. That state had been formed after the northwestern counties of

Virginia had objected to Virginia's seceding from the Union and joining the Confederacy in 1861. West Virginia had been admitted to the Union as the 35th state in 1863. After the war, West Virginia grew quickly, and there was plenty of work on the railroad and in the coal mines. Carter wanted to go with his brothers, but he was still too young to leave home. He continued to work on the family farm. In 1892, when he was seventeen, he joined his older brothers. He wanted to work and save money to go to school.

Carter moved to Huntington, West Virginia, and went to work in the coal mines. He met a black man named Oliver Jones who had fought in the Civil War. Jones operated a tearoom for black workers out of his home. At the end of a hard day laboring in the mines, the workers would gather at his house for ice cream and fruit and to talk and exchange stories. The men were very interested in the news of the day, but few were able to read newspapers. When Jones learned that Carter could read, he offered him free food in exchange for reading the newspapers to his customers. Carter was happy to do so. Much of the talk in Jones's tearoom was about the role of black soldiers in the Civil War. Carter told the story of his father's service with the Union forces. The conversations and the reading he did at Jones's tearoom made him even more interested in learning about black history.

By 1895, Carter's parents had given up their farm and also moved to Huntington, West Virginia. His father got a job working in the railroad building shops. Carter went to live with his parents and enrolled at Huntington's only black high school, Douglass High School. He was older than most of his classmates and eager to catch up, so he studied hard. On Sundays he would go to the railroad shops where his father worked. He would take his father lunch and the Sunday papers, which he would read to him. Many of the railroad workers were Civil War veterans, and the war was often the topic of discussion when Carter visited his father. One Sunday, James Henry Woodson got into a fight with his foreman, a white Confederate veteran. The foreman believed the South had been right in trying to defend slavery and other southern ways of life. After Woodson won the fight, the foreman tried to get him fired. But he was not successful. Carter later said that his greatest learning about the Civil War had come from those who had actually fought in it. He wondered why he had not been taught about the Civil War at Frederick Douglass High School.

Carter completed four years of high-school course work in less than two years. He then entered Berea College in Kentucky. The college had been founded in 1855 for both blacks and whites. At Berea, Carter mixed with whites socially for the first time.

CHAPTER II

TEACHER

Carter Woodson ran out of money after a few months at Berea College. He returned to Huntington and took a job teaching at a school started by black miners for their children. He later served as both a teacher and principal at Frederick Douglass High School. He did not need to have a college degree, only a state teaching license. Woodson earned his teaching license in 1901. He scored between 82 and 91 percent in subjects such as drawing, music, science, and educational methods, as well as history.

Woodson lived with his parents in order to save more of his $65 per month salary for college tuition. He finally graduated from Berea in the spring of 1903— just in the nick of time. The following year the state of

Kentucky outlawed integration in higher education, and Berea stopped admitting black students.

A few months after earning his bachelor of letters degree from Berea, Woodson applied for a teaching position in the Philippines. Those islands had been held by Spain. But Spain handed them over to the United States as part of the treaty that ended the Spanish-American War in 1898. The United States wanted the Filipino people to govern themselves, and the first step was to send American teachers to the islands to train them. Woodson wanted to see other parts of the world. Also, the salary of $100 per month was much more than he was earning as teacher and principal at Frederick Douglass High School.

In November 1903, Woodson traveled to San Francisco, California. There, he boarded the S.S. *Korea* for Hong Kong, in China, and from there took another steamship to Manila, in the Philippines. On that trip, he met a missionary who gave him some important advice. He told Woodson not to try to Americanize his students. They were Filipino. In order to govern themselves, they should study their own language, culture, and history. Woodson agreed with the missionary. It occurred to him that if black Americans were taught more of their own history, they could make more progress in American society.

Woodson was sent to teach in a small town near Manila. His students spoke Spanish, but he spoke only English. He took courses in Spanish that the University of Chicago offered by mail. He also took correspondence courses in French and European history. He used what he learned to teach his students about their own history.

After more than two years in the Philippines, Woodson returned to the United States to visit his parents. He became ill at home and resigned his teaching position in the Philippines. But he was eager to see more of the world. When he was well again, he used the money he had saved to take a trip around the world in 1907. He visited cities in Asia, Africa, and Europe. He visited schools so he could see how students were taught. He went to libraries and read books that he could not get in the United States. He returned home to seek even more formal education.

CHAPTER III

FIRST BLACK PH.D.

Carter G. Woodson wanted to be more than a teacher. He wanted to be a scholar and write books and articles about history. To do so, he had to have advanced degrees. He enrolled at the University of Chicago in the fall of 1907 and earned a master's degree in 1908. He wrote the research paper required to earn that degree on a topic in European history. Woodson then set his sights on a doctor of philosophy (Ph.D.) degree in history. Only a few major universities offered that degree. No black student whose parents had been born in slavery had ever earned one. In the fall of 1908, Woodson won a one-year fellowship at Harvard University in Cambridge, Massachusetts, the oldest college in the nation. Harvard had awarded the first Ph.D. degree to a

18

black American in 1895. That student, William E. Burghardt Du Bois, was from a free northern background.

Woodson did not have an easy time at Harvard. Although the university was one of the few that accepted black students, he was very much alone. Most of the white students believed that blacks were inferior. So did most of the history professors. The first history professor that Woodson studied under did not believe that African Americans had any special history. He dismissed the role that blacks had played in the American Revolution, the Civil War, and American history in general. Woodson was upset by the professor's attitude. He knew from his father's stories, and from the stories of the black coal miners and railroad workers in West Virginia, that blacks had helped the North win the war and end slavery. There were even books written by blacks about the role of African Americans in the Civil War. One was *A History of the Negro Troops in the War of the Rebellion, 1861–1865* by the African-American historian George Washington Williams and published in 1888. Woodson had read that book when he was reading books and newspapers to the black miners in Huntington.

Woodson argued with the professor that African Americans did have a special history. The professor then challenged him to prove his arguments through research. Privately, Woodson promised himself that he would do exactly that one day.

Woodson turned to another Harvard history professor to learn how to do that research. He learned how to find letters, diaries, official records, and newspaper articles, and how to interview people who had witnessed historical events. He also learned how to take the facts he had collected, organize them, and present them in a form that other people could understand.

After a year at Harvard, Woodson still had much more work to do before he could earn his Ph.D. degree. He had to pass a general examination in all his work in European and American history. He also had to write a dissertation, a much longer research paper than a master's thesis. He was not awarded a fellowship for a second year of study, and he did not have the money to pay the tuition.

Carter Woodson made plans to return to the Philippines to teach. He had mixed feelings about returning to those islands. He had enjoyed his time there. But returning would mean giving up his dream for a Ph.D. He could not earn that degree from Harvard through correspondence courses. Just five days before he was to leave, he learned of a teaching job in the black public schools of Washington, D.C. Taking that job would allow him to continue his studies at Harvard.

In the fall of 1909, Woodson started teaching at Armstrong Manual Training High School in Washington. On nights and weekends, he prepared for his general examination at Harvard. As often as he could, he studied at the Library of Congress in Washington. In early 1910, he passed his general examination in European history at Harvard. A year later he took the general examination in American history, but failed.

In the fall of 1911, Woodson was transferred to the M Street High School in Washington. Unlike the manual training school, M Street High aimed to prepare its students for college. It would later be renamed Dunbar High School in honor of the great black poet Paul Laurence Dunbar. Many famous and successful black people would graduate from that school.

Woodson enjoyed teaching at M Street School. He taught many subjects, including American history, French, Spanish, and English. He especially enjoyed teaching American history because he was studying it himself. In April 1912 he took the general examination in American history at Harvard. This time he passed. His dissertation subject was also approved. Woodson wanted to research and write about the formation of the state of West Virginia during the Civil War. He probably would have preferred to write on a subject in African-American history, but most of his professors at

Harvard did not consider such subject matter to be of value.

Woodson did research for his dissertation at the Library of Congress. During the summers he visited his family in West Virginia and did additional research there. He went to county courthouses to study their records. He found and interviewed people who had been alive when the state of West Virginia was formed. In April 1912 his Harvard professors accepted his dissertation. Carter G. Woodson received his Ph.D. degree, the first African American of slave parents to do so.

Woodson was thirty-six years old. It had taken him many years to achieve his goal of obtaining a doctorate in history. But that achievement was not an end in itself. Rather, it was a beginning. Armed with his Ph.D., Woodson intended to prove that African Americans had a long, proud history. He would do studies and publish books and show the world that this was so.

CHAPTER IV

PUTTING BLACK HISTORY "ON THE MAP"

Carter G. Woodson had started writing a book about African-American history even before his dissertation was accepted. His book, *The Education of the Negro Prior to 1861*, was the first of a planned two-part study. He sent it to various publishers but was turned down. The publishers did not believe that enough people would buy the book. They needed to make a profit or at least cover their costs. Finally, Woodson offered to pay for part of the publication costs. G.P. Putnam's Sons accepted the book on that basis, and it was published in 1915. In the book, Woodson told how most blacks had been denied the opportunity for education because of slavery and discrimination. The book received good reviews in the white popular press and historical journals. The first printing had been very small, and in 1919 the publisher issued a second print-

ing of the book. This printing was also small. It did not reach a wide audience.

In 1915, the same year as Woodson's first book was published, an important movie milestone occurred. D. W. Griffith's movie *The Birth of a Nation* appeared. Even today, it is considered a classic of early films. A silent film with on-screen captions that told what the actors were saying, it was accompanied by music in the theaters where it was shown. It was about the Civil War and Reconstruction and was based on the best-selling novel *The Clansman* by a southerner named Thomas Dixon, Jr. The film was filled with the same untruths that Carter had heard from white southerners in the past: That before the Civil War, southern life was perfect and slaves were happy being slaves. That during the Reconstruction period after the Civil War, the former slaves became the puppets of the Union troops stationed in the South. That black men turned savage and attacked white southern women.

The film was hugely popular. Thousands of Americans went to see it. Many believed its untrue version of history. African Americans were insulted by the film's depiction of blacks. The two major civil rights organizations staged marches and other protests against the film. But their efforts were unsuccessful.

Both organizations had been formed just a few years earlier. The National Association for the Advancement of Colored People (NAACP) was founded in 1909 by a group of whites and blacks. The founders hoped to combat the increasing antiblack feeling in the nation. One of them was William E. Burghardt Du Bois, the first African American to earn a Ph.D. from Harvard. The National Urban League was formed in 1910, just one year after the NAACP. It was also formed by both whites and blacks. The Urban League aimed to help the many blacks who were escaping the terrible racism of the South and moving to northern cities.

In the summer of 1915, Woodson went to Chicago to take part in the Exposition of Negro Progress that marked the 50th anniversary of freedom for African Americans. He set up a booth to sell books on black history and posters of famous black people. He and other exhibitors at the exposition talked often about the film *The Birth of a Nation* and its insulting view of blacks. They wished there was something they could do to prove that it was wrong.

As a result of these discussions, Woodson had the idea of forming an organization to promote black history. He believed if the true history of black Americans could be told, blacks would suffer less racism. He believed that a knowledge of their history was the key to their freedom as a people. In September 1915, Woodson led the creation of the Association for the Study of Negro Life and History. He dreamed that it would be a national organization like the NAACP and the Urban League, with branches in many cities and a journal that would be published several times a year.

He realized he faced an uphill battle. Many blacks didn't realize that their history was about more than slavery. They were ashamed of their slave past. Few could afford to give money to national organizations. Those who could preferred to give to civil rights organizations like the NAACP. But Woodson believed that knowledge of their history was key to blacks achieving equality of citizenship in American society.

Woodson set to work on the first issue of *The Journal of Negro History*. He saw the journal as a way to get primary sources on African-American history to the widest audience possible. The first issue appeared in January 1916. Woodson borrowed the money to publish it. He also wrote most of the articles and book reviews. He included letters, diaries, and other original sources. Many of these items were published for the first time in the journal. He also paid attention to the lives of ordinary people. The journal had a continuing section entitled "Undistinguished Negroes." In publishing material about ordinary people, Woodson was way ahead of his time. Several decades would pass before most historians bothered to study the lives of common folk.

The Journal of Negro History was published four times a year. By the time the second issue came out in April 1916, Woodson had set up an office of the Association for the Study of Negro Life and History in Washington, D.C. He held a large meeting in

Washington in August 1917. He invited many white historians, government officials, and wealthy whites who donated money to advance the study of history. At the meeting, he explained that one of the chief aims of the association was "to save the records of the black race." He urged his listeners to spread the word that the documents of black people, famous or not, were valuable. Only through written accounts could the history of African Americans be told from their own viewpoint. Woodson also explained that in order to find and publish those written accounts, the association needed financial support. He planned to hire young historians to do special research projects. But he needed money to pay them for their work. He also needed money to publish the journal. He hoped the people in the audience who could afford to do so would contribute money to his cause.

Woodson invited a number of wealthy whites to serve on a committee he had set up to govern the association. He understood that if they were to give money to support his work, they would want to have a say in how it was spent. But he worried about giving them too much power. He really wanted complete control of both the association and the journal.

In 1917, the same year as the first large meeting of the Association for the Study of Negro Life and History, the United States entered World War I. Three years earlier, Germany had declared war against

Russia and France. Britain and Italy had then joined France and Russia in fighting against Germany. The United States entered the war against Germany in April 1917. Its participation helped ensure the German defeat and surrender in late 1918. Many black Americans enlisted in the U.S. armed forces during the war. Because of racial discrimination, most were not allowed in combat positions. Instead, they built fortifications and served as mess attendants and in other support positions. Their role was not well publicized. Carter understood that racism was the cause.

Woodson believed that the time was ripe for a history of black soldiers. He wrote a proposal for a book and in the fall of 1918 sent it to a number of wealthy whites and asked for money to support the project. At the same time, W. E. B. Du Bois, who edited *Crisis*, the journal of the NAACP, had a similar idea. He asked Woodson to serve as one of the editors on the project. Woodson accepted the invitation. But he asked for more money than Du Bois was prepared to pay. He wanted to do the research himself and have the NAACP support it. He and Du Bois could not come to an agreement.

Woodson did manage to publish, himself, a book about a movement that occurred as a result of World War I. The economic boom that had developed in the United States by the time the nation entered World War I, combined with a halt in the flood of European immigrants into the country due to the war, created labor shortages in the North. Black southerners by the thousands escaped the segregation and lack of opportunity in the South to move to northern cities, where jobs were plentiful. Woodson's short book, published in 1918, put that northern migration in perspective. In that book, entitled *A Century of Negro Migration*, Woodson asserted that the black migration to the North during World War I would prove to be the most important phase in African-American life since the Civil War.

Woodson was still teaching at Armstrong High School. He used part of his own salary to keep publishing *The Journal of Negro History*. Although he managed to sell more than 1,000 subscriptions, he still did not have enough money to support the publication. In 1918 he was offered the job of principal of Armstrong High School, and he accepted with enthusiasm. But he soon learned that his plans to improve the school would not be funded.

In 1919, Howard University invited Woodson to become the dean of its School of Liberal Arts. Located in Washington, D.C., Howard University had been established for black students after the Civil War. The school wanted to create a new graduate program in history. Woodson was delighted to accept. His salary would be higher. He would be able to train younger historians to do the research he believed needed to be done. And the connection with an important African-American university could only help the growth of the Association for the Study of Negro Life and History.

Unfortunately, Woodson lasted only a year at Howard. He soon came into conflict with the new white president of Howard, J. Stanley Durkee. First, Durkee asked him to check and report on whether white members of Howard's faculty were attending a daily chapel service. Woodson felt as if he were a spy. Next, Durkee ordered that a book about the Soviet Union be removed from Howard's library. He did so after a United States senator objected to that book, which presented a positive picture of the Russian Revolution of 1917 and ended with the Communist takeover of the country and the creation of the Soviet Union. Howard University depended heavily on money from the federal government, and Durkee did not want to risk losing that financial support. Woodson was angered by what he considered an attack on free speech. He wrote a letter to the Washington *Star* newspaper attacking Durkee and suggesting that the government should not meddle in Howard's affairs. The letter angered Durkee, who summoned Woodson to his office and berated him.

The two men continued to disagree on important matters, and in June 1920, at the end of the academic year, the board of trustees at Howard fired Woodson. Worried that without a salary he could not keep publishing *The Journal of Negro History*, Woodson asked the NAACP to take over the journal and to pay him to edit it. But the NAACP turned him down.

Woodson was in a quandary. He had big plans, including the creation of a publishing division of the Association for the Study of Negro Life and History. But he could not pursue those plans without money.

Soon, Woodson was offered the job of dean at another African-American college, West Virginia Collegiate Institute. Although he would have preferred to remain in Washington, he accepted the job because the salary of $2,700 a year would help him keep the journal going. While at West Virginia Collegiate Institute, he studied the history of black education in the state. He published the results of his study in *The Journal of Negro History* in 1922. In the meantime, in 1921, he formed Associated Publishers to issue books on black history.

That same year, Woodson's tireless efforts to raise money to support his work finally paid off. The Carnegie Foundation in New York awarded the Association for the Study of Negro Life and History a five-year grant. Beginning in 1922, Carter would receive $5,000 per year to continue his work in African-American history. Not long after receiving the grant, Carter quit his position at West Virginia Collegiate Institute. At last, he could devote himself full-time to his life's work.

CHAPTER V

FOUNDER OF NEGRO HISTORY WEEK

One of the first things Woodson did was to make a down payment on a three-story brick house on Ninth Street in Washington, D.C. The two lower floors would serve as headquarters for the Association for the Study of Negro Life and History. The third floor would be his home for the rest of his life. He spent his days and nights researching and studying black history and presenting to the public what he had learned.

The first book issued by Associated Publishers in 1921 was Woodson's *History of the Negro Church.* Also published that year was a textbook Woodson wrote, entitled *The Negro in Our History*. It filled a great need for books about black history written for young people. Black schools in the South ordered many copies, and it sold out within a year. Revised and updated, a second edition of the book was published in 1923, and seven

more editions followed. The book was not well written, and some of the statements were not supported by facts. But for more than twenty years, it was the best—and practically the only—school textbook on the subject

Also in 1922, Woodson managed to secure another large donation to support his work. The sum of $25,000, also to be paid out over five years, was given by the Laura Spelman Rockefeller Memorial Foundation. This new money allowed Woodson to hire an assistant. There were so many topics in black history that he wanted to research. Now he could assign some of those topics to his assistant. Over the years, many young historians served as assistants to Woodson. He published both their own work and the work they did for him in *The Journal of Negro History* and through Associated Publishers. Carter also worked, less formally, with individuals and groups of young blacks who were interested in African-American history.

In 1926, Woodson announced a national Negro History Week. He chose the second week of February to mark the birthdays of two key men in the struggle for African-American freedom. One was Abraham Lincoln, who as president had freed the slaves. The other was Frederick Douglass, the former slave who had become a leading abolitionist and black leader. Both had been born in February.

Woodson promoted Negro History Week to schools, black clubs, black churches, and other organized groups. He wanted the idea to reach ordinary people, not historians. In the first year, he did little more than prepare a pamphlet that outlined the history of his organization, listed subjects in black history that could be studied, and included a list of important black Americans in history. In later years, he would put together Negro History Week kits for schoolchildren and study guides for adults.

In the same year as he launched Negro History Week, Woodson received the annual Spingarn Medal, awarded each year by the NAACP to honor an African-American who had excelled in his or her field of activity. The award recognized Woodson's tireless efforts to promote black history. The citation that accompanied the award read in part, "For ten years' service in collecting and publishing records of the Negro in America." Just a few weeks later, Woodson was forced to take a two-month leave from his work. He was fifty years old and had struggled for many years, first to earn his Ph.D. in history and then to research and publish material on black history. That struggle had taken a toll on his health.

His illness, and his receipt of the Spingarn Medal, seemed to cause Woodson to think seriously about what would happen to his work if he could no longer do it. He began to seek funds to endow the Association for the Study of Negro Life and History—a large enough sum to ensure that the work of the association would continue without him. He never managed to amass that endowment. The large amount of money he sought was only one reason. A larger reason had to do with his own personality.

Carter G. Woodson was a loner. He never married or even developed any close friendships, and his method of working reflected his private life. He wanted to run a one-man show, to control his organization himself. He did not like even having a board of directors. He did not want to have to answer to anyone else—even to the white foundations that gave him money for his work. He refused to develop a relationship with a college or university because that might mean giving up some control. As a result, even the white foundations that had supported his work in the past became reluctant to continue their support. There would be few additional large grants to the Association for the Study of Negro Life and History.

In the meantime, it was clear to Woodson that much more work needed to be done to put African-American history into American history. In 1928 a white man named William E. Woodward published a biography of Ulysses S. Grant, the Union general who later became president. In that book, *Meet General Grant*, Woodward stated: "The American negroes are the only people in the history of the world, so far as I know, that ever became free without any effort of their own. . . . [The Civil War] was not their business. They had not started the war nor ended it. They twanged banjos around the railroad stations, sang melodious spirituals, and believed that some Yankees would soon come along and give each of them forty acres of land and a mule."

Such continued attempts by white people to deny blacks their proper place in American history infuriated Woodson and made him even more determined to continue his work. In 1933 he published a book entitled *The Mis-Education of the Negro*, in which he attacked the way blacks had been taught in schools. Not only had the American educational system failed blacks in elementary and high school, but it had also failed them on the college level. Woodson charged that African-American colleges also neglected to teach their students about their own history. He believed that the study of black history was an important way to help African Americans be respected, and to respect themselves.

By the early 1930s, Woodson had come to believe that the study of African-American history should go back to the roots of African Americans—to Africa. He began taking summer vacations to Paris, France, where he found a wealth of information on Africa at the National Library of France and in rare-book shops. His ability to read French enabled him to learn and understand far more than if he had relied only on books in the English language. He used the materials he found in Paris to write two books for young people, *The African Background Outlined* (1936) and *African Heroes and Heroines* (1939).

CHAPTER VI

FATHER OF AFRICAN-AMERICAN HISTORY

In an unfortunate coincidence, just at the time when white foundations stopped giving large grants to support Woodson's work in black history, the nation's economy took a plunge. The stock market crash of 1929 ushered in a deep nationwide depression. Banks closed, businesses failed, and millions of people lost their jobs. Blacks, always "last hired and first fired," especially suffered. Few had the money to pay membership dues to the Association for the Study of Negro Life and History. Still, they wanted their children to have a better education than they had, and they did all they could to support their schools. By the time Negro History Week was ten years old, it had really caught on, especially among black schools, churches, and organizations. Woodson continued to develop new suggestions for study topics. In 1937 he started publishing

The Negro History Bulletin. Aimed primarily at schools, the bulletin was published monthly during the school year. It contained photographs and biographical information about important blacks, past and present. Some issues were organized around a theme, such as blacks in art or literature, science or business.

To raise the money to continue his work, Woodson turned to his own people. He organized a Nationwide One-Dollar Sustaining Membership Drive to increase membership in the association and provide operating support. In 1940, when the Association for Negro Life and History was twenty-five years old, he launched a Silver Anniversary Fund and asked for contributions of $25. He raised $7,000.

The association sponsored programs on black history and culture at black colleges, elementary schools, churches, and clubs. Every year, it held an annual meeting at which both scholars and amateur historians lectured on various aspects of the African-American cultural heritage. The programs often included musical performances, art exhibitions, and presentations by black writers, who read from their work.

The United States entry into World War II in 1941 lifted the nation out of the long depression. The war that pitted Germany and its allies against Great Britain and other nations opened up jobs in American war industries for blacks and whites. It also gave African

Americans another chance to serve their country in war. Carter Woodson took the opportunity to put this service in perspective. The February 1944 issue of *The Negro History Bulletin* included an essay he wrote, entitled "My Recollections of Veterans of the Civil War."

Black organizations such as the NAACP pressed the U.S. government to allow African Americans to serve in combat. Under President Harry S. Truman, the U.S. military began to offer more opportunities to black soldiers. Many blacks saw combat in Europe, serving with the forces of America's allies against Germany and its allies. The new United States Army Air Corps (which later became the United States Air Force) started a training school for black pilots. The 99th Fighter Squadron served with distinction in the skies over Europe. Not long after Germany was defeated, President Truman ordered that the U.S. armed forces be racially integrated.

The war, and African-American participation in it, brought about a change in American society. Black soldiers who returned home believed that they had fought to "make the world safe for democracy." They were unwilling to accept anything less than equality at home. Within ten years, African Americans would begin an organized movement to win their rights. The civil rights movement would result in laws granting full legal rights to black Americans.

Carter G. Woodson did not live to see that victorious movement. He died alone at his office/home in Washington on April 5, 1950. W. E. B. Du Bois wrote that Woodson had "kept to one great goal, worked at it stubbornly . . . and died knowing that he accomplished much if not all that he planned." Woodson was hailed as the "Father of Negro History."

The work of the Association for the Study of Negro Life and History went on. In 1970 the word Negro in the title was changed to Afro-American. The term Negro was rarely used by that time. Black or Afro-American were preferred. The association continued to publish its journal, and Associated Publishers kept issuing new books and bringing out new editions of older books. Woodson's 1933 book *The Mis-Education of the Negro* remains in print and selling well. Along with a growing number of black historians—some of whom Woodson had trained—the association continued its pioneering work in black history.

By the 1960s, as American society gradually integrated, black history finally began to be incorporated into American history. Most white historians accepted and highlighted the role of blacks in the history of the nation. Scholarly books and school textbooks featured the contributions of black people. In the 1970s, Black History Week expanded to Black History Month.

Carter G. Woodson and his work have been honored in many ways. In 1974 the National Council for

the Social Studies established the Carter G. Woodson Awards for the most distinguished social-science books appropriate for young readers that depict ethnicity in the United States. In 1975 the house in Washington, D.C., where Woodson had lived and worked was designated a National Historic Landmark. A regional branch of the Chicago Public Library is named for him, and library wings have been built in his honor at the University of Tennessee and the University of Virginia. In 1995 a life-size statue of Woodson was erected on Hal Greer Boulevard in Huntington, West Virginia.

Carter G. Woodson would have been especially pleased about another monument. It had nothing directly to do with him, but it memorialized a cause he championed all his life. In 1998 the African-American Civil War Memorial was unveiled on 10th and U Streets in Washington. It consists of a 3-foot (0.9 meter)-high semicircular stone wall with stainless-steel plaques attached to both sides bearing the names of the soldiers who fought with the U.S. Colored Troops. On this base stands a bronze cast work containing sculptures depicting soldiers from the various armed services on the outer side and a family in the inner circle. The monument stands as a testament to the important role that African Americans played in the war that ended slavery—a role that, thanks in part to the work of Carter G. Woodson, Americans will never forget.

45

BIBLIOGRAPHY

BOOKS

Durden, Robert F. *Carter G. Woodson: Father of African-American History*. Springfield, NJ: Enslow Publishers, 1998.

Goggin, Jacqueline. *Carter G. Woodson: A Life in Black History*. Baton Rouge: Louisiana State University Press, 1993.

Haskins, Jim. *Black, Blue & Gray: African Americans in the Civil War*. New York: Simon & Schuster, 1998.

McKissack, Patricia and Fredrick. *Carter G. Woodson: The Father of Black History*. Springfield, NJ: Enslow Publishers, 1991.

Meier, August, and Elliott Rudwick. *Black History and the Historical Profession*. Urbana, IL: University of Illinois Press, 1986.

Romero, Patricia W. "Carter G. Woodson: A Biography." Ph.D. dissertation, Ohio State University, 1971.

Woodward, William E. *Meet General Grant*. New York: Literary Guild of America, 1928.

ARTICLES

Goggin, Jacqueline. "Carter Godwin Woodson," in Jack Salzman, David Lionel Smith, and Cornell West, eds., *Encyclopedia of African American Culture and History*. New York: Simon & Schuster, 1996.

Logan, Rayford W. "Carter Godwin Woodson," in Rayford W. Logan and Michael R. Winston, eds., *Dictionary of American Negro Biography*. New York: W.W. Norton and Co., 1982, pp. 665–667.

Woodson, C.G., "My Recollections of Veterans of the Civil War," *The Negro History Bulletin*, Vol. VII, No. 5 (February 1944), pp. 103–104ff.

INDEX

47